Notes from a Passage

P.D. St. Claire

"Notes from a Passage," by P.D. St. Claire. ISBN 1-58939-676-6.

Published 2004 by Virtualbookworm.com Publishing Inc., P.O. Box 9949, College Station, TX 77842, US. © 1995, 2004, P.D. St. Claire. All rights reserved. No part of this publication may be reproduced, stored in a retrieval system, or transmitted in any form or by any means, electronic, mechanical, recording or otherwise, without the prior written permission of P.D. St. Claire.

Manufactured in the United States of America.

NOTES FROM A PASSAGE
Introduction

Both of my parents have died, my father in 1982 and my mother five years later. They each lived a good life and with each of their passings we were blessed with a chance to say good-bye. And it was during their passings that I came to realize how little we had actually said to one another over the years, that most of what I learned from them was by things that were done or seen — things shared in common.

And so it is between myself and my children, two boys and a girl. I have coached them in soccer, played football with them, cheered them on in swimming, sweated through exams and science projects, suffered with them the unfairness of teachers and school, anguished with them through bad friendships and the hurts and wonders of self discovery. And in all of this, across the years, few have been the moments that we have truly spoken to each other, when the walls of parenthood were so breached that I could speak with one or another of them as I might a close friend.

The limits of the spoken word were made clearest to me when my oldest son went on a retreat during his junior year at a nearby Jesuit high school. It involved some weeks of preparation and two nights away. Called Kairos, Greek for "God's time," the retreat was a time for each boy to plumb the emerging dimensions of his spiritual life. As parents, our participation was in the form of a letter to our son that would be read aloud to him and the others in the retreat. We were encouraged to express as best we could what he meant to us, the value that he was in our lives. It was not an easy task, but an immensely fulfilling one when done. And as I finished the *letter, I realized that what I had written in it could not easily have been spoken, if at all.*

It is because the spoken word can be so inadequate that we hug one another, that we must sometimes cry to express our joy, that at times we communicate best by silence. But still we must speak. Our children must know who we are and what we value — and why. They must be shown to see beyond the things we give them to make their lives more comfortable. We must pass on what we have learned from our own parents and what we have discovered in our own lives for it is on us as parents to make them better people than they would have been without us — more caring, more loving, less tolerant of the abuse of people and of the doing of evil.

At the end of the day, we must each assume responsibility for our own happiness. As much as we care and as much as we try, we cannot make our children happy. Only they can do that. What we can and must do is to make certain that they see the need to develop and hold values and that the first amongst these is that the life each one of us has been given is sacred and of inestimable worth.

What follows was written first for my children. It is what I believe and have experienced about things that are important to me. It is in writing about them that I have come to a better understanding of them. And it is in writing about them that I hope these things will be shared, that they will be made better and passed on — again.

P. D. St. Claire
Kensington, Maryland
December 1995

Contents

This is life
Water and grass and things that are green
Struck through sheltering trees by a warm morning sun
Yellow in its brilliance

Dogs

HE LIES THERE BEFORE ME ON THE LIVING ROOM FLOOR, his coat warmed by the sun of a brilliant February afternoon. His form raises a measure then falls as a deep breath is taken and released. Stout the dog has been with us for seven full years and though now a member of the family, his coming was not easily managed.

My wife and children had been for some time pressing me to get a dog. Always the practical one, I resisted. (If not me, who?) The children at the time were 14, 11 and 7 — two boys and a girl, respectively. Together on any given day, their mutual proximity threatened to exceed the critical mass needed to achieve a domestic thermo nuclear explosion, especially during the extended closeness of a winter's weekend. The thought of throwing a dog into the mix was beyond imbecilic — it was suicidal, an act of sheer illogicality.

But humans are not generally remembered for their powers of reason; logic is not the stuff of great novels. And my resolve to live a life without a dog fell prey not to the logic of having a dog (there can be none in domesticated society), but to the wonder of my family traveling and reveling for a brilliant summer's week in the hills and valleys of Ireland.

A late evening dinner was the occasion, one following a day absorbed in the emerald lushness of St. Kullum's monastery, a day that closed by the Irish Sea, south of Waterford, at the Haven Hotel. A half dozen Harp beers had settled in my system, their taste and effect heightened by the chorus of revelers singing and carousing in the Hotel's pub as the Irish national soccer team fought England to a draw.

We did not need a dog, that was clear. My position on that was accepted by those at the table, though without sincerity, without conviction, more to allow me an allotted time to speak than to accept my arguments. But the question was not one of need. Children's needs are simple — shelter, clothing, 1,500 calories of food per day, a good friend with whom to play and a parent or other grown-up to challenge or torment. Need had nothing to do with it. Having a dog was a question of want; they all *wanted* a dog, a chocolate Lab, to be precise.

As in diplomacy and poker, the first lesson in child rearing is never to hesitate. Be firm, give nothing, especially when it comes to pets and other living things because you cannot have part of one; there's just no such thing as half a dog. It's an all or nothing event.

It was as dinner was ending and the now eighth or ninth Harp was curing smoothly below that I stumbled, hesitated. Perhaps I was undone by the flash of a memory of the dog in my parents home. His name was Rough of Wildwyn Ramble, a black Lab of kind disposition and manner. He had lived to age sixteen and was put to sleep on a gray winter's morning of long ago to the sadness of all who knew him.

But this warming memory of my childhood dog was of no matter to my wife and children who callously seized upon the resulting hesitation as a pack of jackals would tear at an abandoned calf. One more Harp (ordered by own wife!) was all that it then took and the promise slipped from my lips to be welcomed and made irrevocable by a chorus of cheers and great celebration, all closed by one final Harp. Thus came to our home in the summer of 1988 a chocolate Lab puppy, Stout of Haven Hall. And to my great wonder and delight, the thermo nuclear explosion I had so feared never materialized.

At the core of my concern was the never ending competition among our children for their parents' attention and favor. I have come to view sibling rivalry — no doubt the breeding ground of countless tyrants and despots — as one of the most misunderstood phenomena of raising children. Though it may spark a fight in the wink of an eye, ruining everything from a walk in the park to a Christmas dinner, the root cause for this rivalry is each separate child's need to be loved and it is in needing love that children, eventually, come to understand it and then give it in return. From deep within the reptilian core of the brain that seeks only survival and through the emotional realities of the human condition, the clamor for parental attention is the child's first experience of a social relationship.

It is as these forces play out in the course of a family's development and progress that a dog assumes his most important role. In a world where every slice of pie is scrutinized, every portion of ice cream weighed, where every word or nod of praise will satisfy the one to the alienation of the others, the dog enters, the absolute center of attention, yet wondrously welcomed by all and resented by none. And how can this be explained? In the simplest of terms, a dog is a *non-competing sibling* — a living thing that all can love and cherish without risk of loss, without giving anything up.

Stout became, in fact, a medium of communication among us — among the children, between the children and us, even between us, especially when things were a little off. Each of us, the children especially, could, in loving the dog, love the others without having to express our feelings in so many words. Loving the dog was an act of love that became common to us all and part of each of us.

Of course, such things are rarely even considered when the decision to get a dog is made. Dogs are brought into the home for the children, who almost always abandon them, balking at the simplest tasks, such as pouring a bowl of dry food from a cardboard carton — not to mention attending to the pee and the pooh. Bought to teach a child caring and responsibility, dogs most often teach the parents that their children have neither.

This is not to say, however, that children will not enjoy the dog. As puppies, dogs will seek the excitement of children's screams and gambol and play with them in the yard or wherever strikes their mutual fancy. But in time, a short time, perhaps in less than two hours, the dog will have exhausted the attention of the child and settle on the parents for protection and caring, certainly for regular feeding. Dogs, more obviously than children, know who loves them and to whom to repay the debt. And this is the second service a dog can provide to a family — a dog can be everything that a good child is supposed to be.

Children have responsibilities, even from birth, and first amongst these is to be happy. There is nothing that more reinforces my belief in the ultimate goodness of humankind than this universal need of parents — that their children be happy. Yet it is a need that so often goes unnourished, a need whose frustration can bring the deepest anguish, the greatest sense of loss.

Parents can spend a lifetime chauffeuring to soccer practices and basketball games, then mortgage the farm to pay for an education, even submit to intimidations in their own home lest the child's self esteem be damaged (never mind their own!), yet wait in vain for the slightest sign of happiness. A child's responsibility to be happy appears to be in direct conflict with his right to brood. The most thanks many parents ever get for a well prepared meal is a grunt of appreciation as the child leaves the table to call a friend whom they despise.

Enter the dog. For the price of a Ritz cracker, purchased at fifty to the dollar, a dog's happiness can be assured. And such thanks! Great wags of the tail that shake his entire body and the smile that only a dog can manage with his eyes and ears. Though diminished perhaps by the facility with which such happiness is bought, for a parent struggling to civilize the recalcitrant teenager, it is a welcome respite, an oasis of green and cool waters in a desert bereft of thanks and appreciation.

Then there's the matter of guilt. Being raised an Irish Catholic, guilt is a big part of my life. But this is a taught and learned condition, requiring years of self-absorption and daily confrontations with the near occasions of sin. Guilt does not come easily to today's child. Loved from birth, nurtured with every resource, today's child is fully capable of purposely breaking a thing known to be cherished for the passing pleasure of seeing it crash into thousands of pieces against a hardwood floor. All this and feel not the slightest twinge of guilt or remorse, resisting, even fighting, any instinct to be sorry. Not so the dog. Rough, the dog of my childhood, would not only feel guilt, he would punish *himself.* There was a couch in the living room that was my mother's favorite piece. With pillows and cushions stuffed with the good feathers of some past flock, the couch was a temptation beyond the dog's ability to resist, especially if left

16

alone on a Sunday afternoon.

Now it was not uncommon for us to return home and find him sound asleep on the couch. Cruel as children, we would take great pleasure in waking him rudely and dispatching him to a hated corner in the kitchen where he was forced to sit face-in for some fifteen minutes. There were times, however, when the sounds of our return would wake him before we came into the house. On such occasions, we would find him already in the corner, head hung low, his brown eyes sad, pleading for forgiveness.

Stout's sense of guilt is similar in feeling, if not as dramatic in expression. No sumptuous couch for him; Stout's weakness is the kitchen garbage bag. (Though also pedigreed, Stout's forebears would appear to have been of a lesser station than Rough's.) When caught in the bag, sometimes beyond his ears, he will quickly retreat. Half squatting with his forelegs, he cravenly sleeks to his place of punishment and protection — under the dining room table where I can land only a glancing blow, and this at risk of breaking my hand on the arm of a chair or the leg of the table. No matter, really. My need is not to punish the dog. My need is an acceptance of guilt, an expression of remorse, and a dog can provide these to the needing parent in unlimited quantities.

Weaning is next. In studies of the *familia humanis,* much is made of weaning. First from the breast, then from the hearth, the focus is always on the child. Well, weaning is a two way event and a dog can be of great assistance to parents passing through it. Despite the fact that a child will spend years in a desperate competition with his siblings for the attention of a parent, a time will come when he wants to disappear completely from a parent's view, never mind being actually touched by one. A dog, on the other hand, will never tire of being petted. Stout, now 49 in dog years, has a particular weakness for having his ears stroked and his jowls worked. To the parent in need of the most basic medium of expression, the touch, a dog can be a most agreeable surrogate.

And there's more. We all have fantasies, or should have I suppose, and for some time one of mine was to be able to talk to Stout, to hear what he had on his mind. I've come away from that now. The reason goes to an afternoon drive listening to the tape of The Three Tenors in Rome — Pavorati, Domingo and Carras. Toward the end of the concert, several songs are done in English. To my surprise, the pleasure taken is diminished. The explanation, I have come to believe, is that the beauty of the voices is obscured by the meaning of the words.

And so with Stout. In not being able to speak with him, I am left only the beauty of his soul, the completeness of his being, undiminished by the structure and mechanics of language. His presence is enough, his form lying in the sunlight on a cold winter's day, content and at peace.

LEADERS

I GREW UP IN BAY SHORE, NEW YORK, on the south shore of Long Island. Bay Shore had prospered after the war as the domicile of lawyers, stock brokers and other executives who each morning boarded the Long Island Railroad for the outside world — New York City, forty-five miles to the west. Each day these men traded stocks, managed companies and wrote the briefs that earned the money that bought the food and clothing and paid for the plumbers and electricians and otherwise drove the economy of the town.

I left Bay Shore for Washington, DC, in January 1968 to take a position with the Central Intelligence Agency, marrying in that city four years later. My wife and I regularly returned to Bay Shore to visit, though, and during one of these visits, I think it was in the late 1970s, something occurred that always comes to mind when I think about leadership.

It was at St. Patrick's Church, the 9 a.m. Sunday mass. I was dressed in a navy blazer, gray flannel pants and a camel overcoat. With my horn rim glasses and hair cut short, I could easily have passed for a lawyer or a stock broker — one of those who brought in the money from the outside world. At the part in the Mass where the peace offering is exchanged, I turned to the person at my right, a woman, and offered my hand. I sensed that she had been looking at me. She did not immediately respond. I smiled, gestured again with my hand. "Peace," I said.

She offered her hand and, as our hands touched and she spoke the word "peace", she bowed. It was barely a movement of the head and neck, but it was definitely there — a bow. For a

19

moment, it made me uncomfortable, though she did not seem to notice this as she turned away to offer her hand to the person on the other side of her.

I never saw the woman again. By her face and complexion, I took her to be of Irish descent. Judging by her clothes, she did not drive her husband to the station for the commute to the city each morning. Her husband made his way to a machine shop, or the gas works or as a carpenter to a house a-building. By her gesture, though, the woman saw me as a leader and herself as a follower.

It would be easy to dismiss what the woman had done as the act of a person who was intimidated by my appearance and assumed herself to be from a lower social station. But there was something in the way she looked at me that said much more. It said that she understood me to know more than she did and on the basis of this she structured a relationship between us. It was not, by her look, a relationship that she regretted or one in which she feared exploitation. Quite the opposite.

The woman sensed that I knew better than she where Bay Shore was in relation to other places on the planet and how the things that she needed to survive came to be made available to her. If a problem developed, it was I to whom she would turn to have it fixed. Since I understood better how the world worked, I was responsible for ensuring that it worked well. In this relationship that she so quickly assumed, it was I who was the burdened party. And so it is with a society's leaders.

We often think of leadership in the context of structures and their management. And in these structures, there are processes by which a person rises through the ranks — the manager becomes the director, the director the VP, the VP becomes the Executive VP who becomes the President and CEO. All this because each structure must have someone at its top. Those at the top of these structures are presented to us as leaders — and though many of them are, many are not.

It is for this that we must understand the difference between a leader and a manager. Where the leader is internally directed, a manager must look to others for direction. Where the leader motivates by example or by force of personality, a manager assigns tasks and monitors progress on their completion. Where the leader assumes, takes to himself, the authority to achieve a goal, a manager is given authority by another and accepts instruction in its application and use. Where the manager is satisfied with the correct answer, the leader is not satisfied until he has found the right question.

A leader does not seek followers as much as he is sought by them. A leader is goal-oriented, not necessarily people oriented, and these goals are generally beyond complete expression in quantifiable or even personal terms. In being goal oriented, the leader attracts to himself those who are less so, people whose energies seek expression in the achievement of a goal which they are unable to identify or to specify.

The structures that manage most of what gets done in this country are orderings of human capital done largely on the basis of knowledge, intelligence, measurable achievement and conformance with tradition. But leadership must be more than these. Leadership has to do with determining what the structures will do — how the resources of the structures will be applied and to what end. Even more, leadership has to do with ensuring that the structures serve the purposes for which they were created and, more fundamentally, that these purposes remain good.

While everyone senses the need for a leader, not everyone can be one. Though we are encouraged from birth to see ourselves as leaders, the reality for most of us must be to assume the role of the follower. Sorting this out as we grow up can be difficult. In fact, if there is a single measure of a person's maturity, it may be this; that he has come to understand that leadership is the interaction of the leader and the led and has settled on which one of the two he is. In coming to understand that leadership is the relationship between the leader and the led, each understands that the informed, mature follower is more than a part of the whole, he is essential to it. It can not exist without him and in this he finds his value, his contribution.

Most of what has gone badly in history can be laid at the feet of false leaders. The false leader's gift is not in having a vision, but in exploiting what others covet or fear. His achievements are measured in control, not empowerment; in owning, not shar-

21

ing; in division, not unity; in what will dissolve, not endure; in hate, not in love. The false leader's energies are spent on securing a *status quo* that serves his personal needs and desires. Such people are not leaders, they are bullies, and in their wake lies the misery of millions who have been betrayed by them.

A true leader is a change agent, a person who from birth or through life has come to understand that the *status quo* is an oxymoron, that there is simply no such thing. Every minute we are older and, each day, forces and events change history and redefine our future. The world is in constant motion. While others may not even be aware of this, leaders assume it.

It is in knowing that change is inevitable that leaders seek change for a purpose, for the better. Inside the leader there is an instinct, a drive, even a calling, that resists entropy — the degradation of all matter and energy to an ultimate state of inert uniformity. Leaders confront the pull of gravity of lesser men, those who never seek to live beyond the life that fate and chance have dealt them. And so it is that those who follow are not so much in the service of their leaders as they are in their debt.

For all its faults, the world is a far better place in which to live today than it was fifty years ago, or a hundred years ago or two hundred or a thousand. What has been achieved has not been done by the whining and the moaning of the masses, but by leaders who saw a better world and had the courage to take us to it. And so it rests on each of us neither to whine nor to moan, but to learn and to know when to lead and when to follow — and then to do it.

LIES

I WENT TO CHAMINADE HIGH SCHOOL in Mineola, New York. It was named in honor of Fr. William Chaminade, founder of the order of priests and brothers who teach there to this day.

Fr. Chaminade lived in France during the post-Napoleonic era, a time when the "Daughter of the Church" was going through something of an identity crisis. Anti-clericalism was rife in the land and fewer and fewer young Frenchmen were answering God's call to the religious life. As might be imagined, it was a particularly difficult time to start a religious order.

Adversity, though, has a way of breeding legends, heroes of danger and daring. Despite the times, Fr. Chaminade did start his order, the Marianists, and the good brothers regularly regaled us with tales of his struggles against the forces of evil and atheism. One was told with particular relish.

It seems that one afternoon Fr. Chaminade, dressed as a common traveler, was walking along the road to Lille. When stopped by soldiers with a warrant for his arrest, he was challenged as to the whereabouts of "the priest, Chaminade." The Founder replied that he believed that Chaminade traveled the road to Lille, motioning in the direction of the city as he spoke. Taking this to mean that Chaminade was ahead of them on the road to Lille, the soldiers galloped off in pursuit of the man with whom they had just spoken.

So clever, the Founder! He had escaped the soldiers without having told a lie! Small wonder the order he founded had prospered!

Well, as a teenager struggling with logic and emotion to

23

set my moral compass, I found the story somewhat perplexing. If a lie is an act meant to deceive the person to whom it is directed then had not the Founder lied? He may have spoken a fact, but that does not mean he did not speak a lie. Better he had told the soldiers to buzz off and take his chances with the law than leave this story to his followers to confuse generations of hapless school boys as yet unaware that a fact can be made into a lie.

For most of us, a lie is our first sin, our first immoral act. George Washington aside, we have all told lies and are likely to do so again as we work our way through the mine fields of personal and professional relationships. But as with sins in general, lies come in different sizes and with varying consequences — for teller and tellee, alike.

Consider this scenario. A vase is broken. No one, save the boy responsible, actually saw the event transpire, knows for certain that it was he who had lost his balance in pursuit of an imaginary pirate and knocked the vase to the floor. Conveniently, there lives in the house a dog and two cats. Now picture the 3' 1" child confronted by the 6' 2" father and who has been taken from his work. The question booms: "Who knocked over the vase?" The answer is obvious; "The dog — or the cats..."

It is, in fact, hardly a matter of morals at all. Imagine yourself confronted with an 12' 4" giant with an attitude, his nostrils glaring, his shadow about to envelope you, blotting out all light and seeming to knock askew the very axis of the earth. Implicating the ever ungrateful cats or a flea infested dog would not be so much a lie as an act of inspired self-preservation. More precisely, the boy spoke a defensive lie, one told to cover the unintended consequence of an otherwise innocent act. If there is a lie with which we can all feel some sympathy for the teller, surely it is this one.

As we grow older, however, occasions increasingly present themselves for lies of an offensive nature. Unlike the defensive lie, the offensive lie is told to gain an undeserved advantage — perhaps an extra ration of food or a warmer place to sleep. The point is, though, that the objective sought is valid and is, in and of itself, a good. While morally the end can never justify the means, surely the fact that the end for which the lie was told was not a bad thing should account for something.

Not so other lies, darker acts, lies told to hurt someone. Such lies have no benefit to the fabricator beyond the pleasure of someone else's discomfort or loss. Because of this, because their goal is to achieve a harm, they are far worse than lies told to achieve a good. The people who tell such lies step beyond the defense of self-preservation, or of even self-promotion, and enter into the realm of the perverse. The only service such lies offer mankind is to remind us that the worst thing about a lie is that to tell one, you first must know the truth.

There are also lies told by persons on behalf of organizations — governments, corporations, groups of people and social structures. These can be lies of commission or omission and are generally justified on the basis of a greater good. Rarely unfactual, they often skirt an issue rather than confront it and are generally employed to gain time to set a matter straight, or to just stall in hope that the other party will lose interest and go away. Diplomatic lies fall into this category. Often told to bridge a gap in time, they can serve to avoid an unwanted or unneeded confrontation. Since both sides understand the game at play and there is no deceit of significance or intention to harm, it is arguable that there can be little moral sanction.

And, of course, any discussion about lies and the telling of untruths must include some consideration of the most common genre — *bullshit* and those who purvey it, the ever present bullshitter. A species known to every culture and caste, the bullshitter comes in numerous types, of which I shall dwell on but two — Type-A and Type-B.

The Type-A bullshitter can usually be sighted leaning against the bar at the local watering hole nattering nonsensical platitudes about athletes, living and dead. Typically, the discussion focuses on deeds done and records set, seen either in person with "my own eyes" or related first-hand by someone (often a blood kin) who was "on the plane back from the game."

Apart from the continuing depletion of his own self-esteem, such a person is as harmless as a bad song except that the standard size and deportment of the Type-A bullshitter (XX suit coat and clumsy) might some day impede the access of the others in the bar to the fire exit.

The Type-B bullshitter may charitably be described as an

errant optimist. Differentiated from the Type-A by the level of his mischief, the potential harm of the Type-B bullshitter can generally be measured in direct proportion to his actually having achieved something of note in an earlier life on which he now trades.

The Type-B can get two or three investors in a room, regale them with one near fact after another and never himself actually lie — that is, never intend to deceive them any more than he is deceiving himself. Unable to actually produce as much as he himself consumes (which is usually a lot), the Type-B is condemned to see anyone's gain as some else's loss. The idea of someone actually producing more than he consumes is totally foreign to him. Although the Type-B can be entertaining, we engage him at the risk of our time, our money and our own self-esteem.

While the Type-B bullshitter is of minor consequence in the great scheme of things, he helps us to see that deception is a two-party event. How often do lies go unchallenged because those hearing them will not risk the displeasure of those telling them? But the displeasure of such people is no great calamity. Of what value or worth could be the company and approval of a *liar*?

To have meaning, life must be a search for truth. And while you may not always be able to see the truth in a thing, with courage and honesty, you can always see the lie in a thing.

GIFTS

I WAS SECOND BORN IN A FAMILY OF FIVE, four boys followed by a girl. Our births were spread over ten years — 1941 through 1951 — and, despite spates of sibling rivalry, we have become close over the years.

One of the more poignant moments of my early childhood was the discovery that my older brother had my father's name. My age on coming to know this was three or four, sufficiently young to be standing behind my parents in the rear of the family car. My father was driving; I was behind him and could see my mother in profile on the passenger side of the front seat.

Until that morning, I was not aware that my father had a name other than *Daddy* or *Dear*. His having a name like any other person was disappointing; it diminished his uniqueness, his authority. But more startling than the fact the he had a name was that his name was the same as that of my older brother — John. On learning this, I turned immediately to my mother to learn her real name, hoping that it was the same as mine. It was Moira. No help. I was alone.

Getting your father's name is one of the advantages of being the firstborn son. In year's past there were others — some more substantial. Under the common law holding of *primo geniture,* the firstborn son got everything when the father died. Now there's a *real* advantage. In more recent times, when a son was still expected to enter his father's business, the firstborn got a leg up on the rest by reason of being first introduced and trained to it. Today, though, in a world where fairness is legislated at every turn, in a world where knowledge is king and anyone with a brain can get it, the advantage of being firstborn has greatly diminished. In fact, it may have come the other way around.

Today, the first born is the source of parental angst beyond the capability and culpability of any child that may follow. Every step and stage is new ground for both parent and prodigy. As with the Hippocratic oath, parents feel bound first "to do no harm." Caution is the watchword. Be right. It's too important a thing, raising a child, to screw up — you could ruin a life, a *whole goddam life!*

For the first born, there is no sibling at hand who knows the ropes. No one who can say, "Listen, kid, it's allright. They're just a little nervous, that's all. Relax, they'll calm down. In an hour or so, no one will even remember you nearly fell a hundred feet to your death chasing a ball on the Billy Goat Trail." For the first born, there's no buffer, just him and a twenty-eight year old woman and a thirty-year old man, both of whose lives have been irretrievably changed, if not ruined, not to mention two sets of grandparents, assorted in-laws and the entire western world looking on in judgment. Absent *primo geniture,* being first born could well be more burden than benefit.

Which is not to say that life's all cake and ice cream for the second son. For one thing, there's 18 years or so of playing catchup, near two decades of the first son being faster, stronger, smarter, "...erer" in just about everything except victimization. And my older brother was all of these things and more. A good athlete, he was possessed of an unfailing desire to win and was uncommonly strong-willed.

I am not certain the degree to which my relative ineptness in most things contributed to this behavior in my brother. (Talk about victimization!) What I do know is that on one of the few occasions that I bested him in wrestling — had that sucker pinned to the floor, face down in a hammer lock, ramming his right hand up to the near vicinity of his left ear — his only response was a vow that as soon as I let him up, he was *really* going to kick the shit out of me! What do you do with a guy like that?

An older brother does have his uses, though. Apart from breaking-in your parents, he'll look out for you. Also, if your older brother has amounted to anything at all in school or on the playground, you'll generally get the nod over others of whom absolutely nothing is known when teams are picked. An older brother can also be a source of information, expand your own horizons.

My older brother went to Holy Cross College in Worcester, MA. He was there introduced to the Jesuits and studied under a traditional curriculum with which he was quite comfortable and from which he learned a great many things. It was in this environment that he first encountered the Don Cossack Chorale — survivors of the White Army that had tried unsuccessfully to topple the Bolsheviks in the early years of Communist Russia. From its forming in the 1920s until its passing some years later, the troop traveled throughout Europe and North America, singing songs of home, of Russia, of fields and streams, and of quiet walks with a girl friend.

It was during a Christmas vacation while we were both in college that he first shared his discovery with me. He checked out a Don Cossack album from the local library and we listened to it together on a cold and wet afternoon. There is an edge to the singing that no matter the lyric has the ring of men far away, making ready for campaigns and war, caught between the pull of home and sweethearts and the glory and adventure of battle. But the mood is never militaristic. Throughout the singing there is the sense of ordinary men joined in common cause, in love with their country, bound as one to a coming fate.

What my brother liked most was the whistler. Throughout the songs, one of the Chorale would break out in a chorus of whistling, the sound soaring above the voices like a freed eagle, finding a singular height, yet always complementing the others, giving meaning and definition to the voices below. I think my brother identified with the whistler, someone who had managed to free himself from the pack without really leaving it, some one who banged off the others, challenged them without threatening them. He is like that, looking for the twist, the juice in life.

Some years later, after I had left home and moved to Washington, I came across an album of the Red Army Chorus. It had to be the same music, I reasoned, and bought it. And the music was the same, right down to the whistler. Led by Col.

Boris Alexandrov, son of the unit's organizer, Alexander Alexandrov, the songs would pull at any soul, rhythms that come through our ears and seem to release something already inside of us that more than makes us free, that takes us beyond our sense of needing to be.

Several years ago, as the Soviet Bloc was dissolving before an incredulous world, the Red Army Chorus was on a world tour with a stop in Washington. Col. Alexandrov had since passed from the scene, but the show was nonetheless masterful, complete with a moving rendition of *Shenandoah,* a rousing *Le Marseilles* and a choreographed depiction of US and USSR armies linking up at the end of World War II. Schmaltzy, to be sure, but the Russians always manage to pull it off. It was a wonderful experience.

After the show, cassettes by the Chorale were being sold in the lobby. I bought two, one for me and one for my brother. I had no idea the last time he had listened to the Don Cossacks or whether he had ever even heard of the Red Army Chorus, but I thought he'd like it and sent the cassette in the mail.

It was a good gift, perhaps the perfect gift. It returned to someone else what he had given to me — the songs of Russia, of a people, the sense of an entire culture. It reminded my brother of something he liked and, hopefully, of an afternoon we had spent together many years before. It told him that he had given me something that had grown in me over the years and was good. He would now have the pleasure of listening to the music and the comfort that there was something more at play — there was our relationship that after so many years was not only alive but still growing.

Gifts, like so many things, can become less than they could be. Not a month goes by that there is not some structured occasion — obligation, even — to give a gift. Often it is just payback for an earlier favor or a social debt to the child of an inanimate cousin who makes a practice of remembering your child's birthday but hasn't had a nice talk with you in years. Gifts can clutter a wedding feast and stuff an otherwise useful closet. They can become so anticipated as to be anticlimactic. Worse still, a poorly chosen gift can easily do more harm than good.

But gifts can be wonderful. They can reinforce new relationships and make old relationships new. The urge to give a gift can lift us from a funk, rescue us from a bad day. We should not let such feelings pass by. We must be willing to take a chance that the person would like a gift from us, that they like us. We should bend to those feelings inside each of us that reach out, that call us to share our lives with other people. In gifts, it truly is the thought that counts.

Recently, I visited New York and had the occasion to ride in my brother's car. Behind the right front passenger seat there was a pocket for odd things that he had filled with cassettes to listen to as he traveled the roads of Long Island in his law practice. I reached in and pulled out the cassette laying on top. Scratched and scarred from use and play, I could just barely make out the title — The Red Army Chorus, Alexander Alexandrov, founder.

Of all the gifts I have given in my life, none had been more rewarding than this. It was nice to see that it was still giving.

BIGOTS

THERE IS THE STORY ABOUT THE BLACK MAN in Mississippi who took it upon himself to vote. The year was 1954. He had been born sixty years earlier. His father, a free man from Ohio, had fought in the Civil War, and had married the man's mother in 1883. She had been born a slave.

The man stood just under six feet with white hair cut short and receding off the forehead. Excusing himself from work, he started for the polling place at mid-afternoon dressed in a pair of dark trousers and a plaid shirt that hung easily over his full shoulders. He had put in overtime in his job as janitor at the town hall for the five dollar poll tax.

The polling place was the Veterans of Foreign Wars headquarters, just off the town square. Originally built as a school house, the building was of red brick with a tin shed roof over the front porch where the registrar sat in the shade of the afternoon sun. As the voters stepped up to the porch, he greeted them, checked their names against a list and then and gave them forms with which to vote. It was hot for November, with much fanning of themselves by the several women in the line.

The man approached the line and took a place at the end of it. His appearance seemed to raise the temperature still further, with the women in line working their fans more feverishly and the men pulling at their collars more frequently. Most had known Charles their whole lives and they were surprised by his appearance. Some seemed angered, others disappointed, even hurt. Charles was a good man — reliable, never made trouble. Charles was a colored who would seem to have known better.

Those joining the line after Charles stepped in front of him. Some gave the air of doing this on purpose, while others seemed to do it unconsciously, as a matter of course. And there were still others who, by their looking about and hesitating, gave the appearance of doing so because it would not sit well with the rest if they had not. As the afternoon wore on and there were fewer and fewer people to step in front of him, Charles steadily moved forward toward the table, finally coming to it just before the polls were to close.

The registrar was a man in his fifties. He wore a thin black tie tied tight against the collar of a faded short sleeved shirt. A wide brimmed khaki hat covered his head. He looked around Charles, perhaps to see if there was a white man in line behind him. Avoiding Charles' eyes, he then surveyed the area in front of the building. After a pause, he looked up. "What you want, boy?" he said, as if distracted from his duty, from something important

Charles raised his head a measure, not taking his eyes off the man. "To vote," he said.

"You say vote, boy? Vote?" The man's voice rose as he half came up from his chair. His point made, he sat back down and began to busy himself with some papers on the table. After a moment, he began to speak in a lower voice. "Now what you want to do that for, Charles? Who you gonna vote for, anyway? Ain't no colored running. What difference it make to you what white man wins?"

"Here's my five dollars," Charles said. "I want to vote."

"Now hold on, boy," the man said, now loud enough for those watching to hear. "You can't just walk up here, throw down five dollars and say 'I want to vote.' We got rules here, boy, PRO-cedures. What you think this is, some kind of banana republic?"

"No, sir," said Charles. "I just want to vote. You got my five dollars."

"Well, boy," the man said, "here in Mississippi, we can't just have anyone come up here and say who's going to run the place. You got to qualify, boy."

"How do I do that?'

"Well, it being that it's so late, I might wave the rule on registration. But, by God, boy, you got to show me you can understand what's going on around here, you got to show me you can read." The man sat back in his chair, spat to his right, then looked back up at Charles. "You read, boy?"

Charles paused for a moment, then said, "Yes, sir, I can read." He looked at the newspaper on the table beside the man. "Says there that Mr. President Eisenhower coming down to Augusta to play golf next week."

The man sat up, looked at the paper, folded it over as if it was something that Charles should not have seen. "Hell fire, boy," he said, sitting forward against the table. "I'm not talking about sports! What jackass can't read the sports? We got a world of trouble out there, boy, and I got to be sure you know what's going on in it before I can let you vote for the folks that's going to be running it." He reached behind him into a box and pulled out several newspapers. "Here," he said, "read this."

Charles took the offered copy of *Le Monde.* He studied it carefully for a minute before pointing to the headline and reading it aloud in French and then translating it into English. "Says here that M. Jean Monet gonna start up a European Economic Community."

The man paused for a moment, looked at the paper then back at Charles. "Do it, now?" he said. He picked up another paper and handed it across the table. "I guess then you can tell me all about this, too."

The copy of *Allgemeiner Zeitung* was yellowed and frayed at the edges. Charles held it back for his eyes to focus on the print and began to read aloud in German before translating into English. "The German economy is expected to continue to grow at 8+% for the next two quarters."

The man's eyes locked on Charles as he reached for a third paper that he handed over as he spoke. "We don't got to worry none about them fellas in Europe, boy. Hell, we licked the Germans twice and the French a bunch of sissies." He let a smile crack his lips as he nodded to the third paper. "Why don't you tell me about the rest of the world, boy, the places where all our enemies are?"

Charles had never seen a Chinese newspaper before. He held the copy of the *People's Daily* back from his eyes, as he had done before, and studied the characters. After a moment, he pointed to the top of the front page as he spoke in a deliberate, measured tone. "Now I'm not too sure 'bout this here Chinese, boss," he said. "But I do believe the headline says 'Ain't no colored voting in Mississippi this year.'"

Ethnic stories are part of our every day lives. Some are vicious, some less so. Truth be told, the less vicious seem to relieve a secret, unknown pressure inside many of us. The story about Charles is even benign. It's about one man holding on to what dignity is available to him in a culture of prejudice. By every measure of value, Charles is superior to those who would deny him the right to vote. It is they who are the less for day, even though Charles must return to the backroom of the town hall, still unrepresented by the government he serves.

Bigotry has many roots. Ironically, its seeds can be sown by those closest to us, by those who love us most dearly. In the name of safety, we are raised to avoid things that are different from the things we know, to be afraid of them. Our parents do this for our well being, to keep us safe from the unknown and the seemingly unknowable.

We must also remember, too, that we are physical things and that our first information about the world around us is of a physical nature. We are rewarded in school for seeing the differences between physical things; it is one of the ways our intelligence is measured. Rising above bigotry requires us to overcome what we first see in a thing or a person, to go beyond the physical information that our eyes and ears bring to our brain and to engage our human mind.

Bigotry has been with us since the dawn of time. It is made of fear and ignorance, selfishness and hatred. These are its building blocks. At its core, bigotry is a perversion. It denies that we are more than the type body we each have been issued, that thing in which our human spirit dwells. It insists that a black man or a yellow man or a white man or a red man is somehow less than a man. And in denying one man equality, equality is denied to all, literally and in fact — completely. Ironically, bigotry's ultimate effect on the human spirit is to consume the host in which it lives. While bigotry unchecked will make more difficult — or even destroy — the lives of those against whom it is directed, it more certainly destroys the souls of those who practice it.

There are few of us who are above bigotry in one form or another. Clearly, we are all tempted by it — to seize an easy, unearned advantage, to feel superior by right of color or caste, to exercise the power of exclusion. Those who fall to this temptation will even cite scientific studies in their cause. And the longer they persist in their prejudice, the more it seems to control them. Ultimately, though, bigotry must be seen for what it is — a sin against our fundamental need to be with others, against the potential and the reality of the unity of humankind. If love's sin is hate, then the unity's sin must be bigotry.

As with any sin, bigotry will always be with us. It is beyond the great majority of us to avoid some measure of it. What is not beyond any of us, though, is to recognize that it is evil and something that we should strive to overcome. At a minimum, our goal must be to be less of a bigot than those who went before us and to work so that those who follow us are less bigoted than are we.

If we can have done that, we will have done a lot.

PARANOIA

Guard against it
Life is tough enough dealing with the
People who *are* out to get you

FRIENDS

I GAVE UP DRINKING SOME YEARS AGO. The decision to do this had its roots in a multi-mirrored hotel bathroom in Geneva, Switzerland. While shaving after a morning shower, I had caught sight of my hind quarter in one of the mirrors and literally took it to be someone else's. The bulk of the thing and its general condition could be described only as in surplus. Something had to be done and a non-drinking diet was the quickest, surest step.

It had not been my intention to give up drinking completely — just for the month of January. However, something had been at work inside of me for a while, something that kept saying in quiet undertones that drinking was unhealthy for me. (This voice spoke sometimes in louder tones, thundering pulses at the temple and across my forehead on a Sunday morning for which the only discovered quieting was great quantities of carbonated soda and the passage of time.) In any event, I felt so much better at the end of the month than at the beginning that I just quit altogether.

But nothing is without cost or consequence, and so with this. I soon discovered that my not drinking was a problem for some of my friends. And as their disquiet (poorly concealed in words of faint praise) continued into that spring, I came to conclude that the only real drinking problem many people may ever have is friends of theirs who think it's a problem that they don't drink.

But I am ahead of myself.

It was during that February, at one of my second son's basketball games, that I came to think about friends and friendship. Mounting the bleachers as I bundled my coat to use as a cushion, I came to sit next to a neighbor of some ten years. He smiled, I smiled back, we exchanged pleasantries about the weather and other things that came to mind. For the first time in our relationship, I realized that he had passed from being just someone I knew to being a friend. It relaxed me completely.

Now, since not drinking was regularly on my mind, it occurred to me that this is what one gets from drinking with friends — relaxation, a letting go of the boundaries we build around ourselves. But I had now come to realize that you don't have to drink anything to achieve it; just being with a friend can do the trick. What is more, I came to see that when people, especially men, go out to drink, what they are really doing is going out *to friend*. It's when the drinking becomes more important than the friending that the problems begin. The simple fact is that you can drink alone, but you cannot friend alone.

It is in raising children, though, that friends are best appreciated. I am not talking about the support we seek from our friends as we work to be good parents, but about the friends of our children. Among the things that I hold most dear are my children's good friends. And though I am blessed with children who have chosen good friends, I believe that I can appreciate the anguish of parents whose children have not. A bad friend will pull a child away from the family's center, challenging the values that a parent works to instill. As any caring parent learns, if your children have good friends, you're halfway home.

The friendships of childhood, however, can break down as we grow older. Often built on physical proximity, the bonds of youth give way to differences in ability and instinct, in taste and need. Yesterday's friend can become today's weirdo. Men seem more prone to this phenomenon, less likely to have friendships that last a lifetime. Women, for their part, seem to hold friends longer and dearer. Truth be told, a woman's best friend often rivals her husband in importance — and is all but certain to outlive him.

That broad slices of the male population fail to have meaningful mutual relationships is perhaps best marked by the surge of "male bonding" that swept across the country in the 1980s. It seemed for the yuppie generation that just plain ol' being with the guys didn't quite cut it. A spin was needed, something to make it more grown up, more sophisticated, more socially acceptable, and male bonding was the answer.

Under the cover of "bonding" with fellow males, otherwise reluctant professionals could express their need for the company of other men without the commitment that a relationship with a *friend* might entail. Though a step in the right direction, it was faulted because it allowed the "bonders" to treat friendship as another function, as an element of their lives rather than as an emotion. In doing so, "bonding" debased the need for friendship and likely frustrated the goal it was supposed to achieve.

Bonding aside, there is something in men that drives them to be independent of other people. For many men, a friend is someone to bounce off of, to compete with, a companion against whom teeth and paws are tested. Real men are tough. They don't eat brie and can live fulfilled in the wild — alone — for months at a time. In male society, a man will mark his place by what he can make or produce, will see his utility in relative terms and by this fix his place among other men.

There is a fear in this fixing, though. For some, defining themselves relative to others can lead to a loss of self, a loss of independence. And as we fix ourselves among those around us in the world of business and commerce, we deny ourselves those places held by the others. We accept a station and this can grate on a person not yet ready or able to deal with his own limitations.

It is common among men to challenge one another's success and to pick at a weakness. Beneath the surface, there is a reluctance to congratulate from the heart, a hidden hope that another will fail, or at least have the common decency not to excel. The Germans have a phrase for it; *schadenfreude* — the secret delight in a friend's misfortune. A man's keeping this inside may make him seem less catty than a woman, but it is none the less there and, since hidden, the more threatening to a good friendship.

But even in less than perfect friendships there is something in wanting and having friends that fulfills us, that confirms that we need each other, something that tells us we are part of one another. Ultimately, there is a force inside each of us that draws us toward a unity with those we see around us, an un-written law of human gravity. While we pull against this force as it may seem to threaten our independence, in the end this is wasteful and fruitless. And even if we could succeed in denying this force, our reward is a life apart from those we see around us, a life alone.

We can best express love — our most compelling need and most complete act — with and through others. Though everyone wants to be free, nobody wants to be alone. Bridging these needs and forces is what friendship is all about. It's what good friends are really for.

HABITS

Develop good habits
They will free you to do
The more important things

$HOWS

OUR SECOND TELEVISION SET had a twelve inch screen built into a blond ash cabinet that stood about three feet tall. The speaker was in the bottom half behind wooden lattice work fixed over beige muslin. I believe that it was a Motorola. I am certain that it cost $247.

The year was 1950 and I was in the second grade. The reason I am so certain about the price is that it prompted the first question I can remember having of an economic nature. To wit: How did the $247 get from Mr. Barrett's appliance store on Main Street in Bay Shore to Howdy Doody in New York? And more important, how far would the $247 go with Buffalo Bob, Clarabell and the guys running the puppets to be paid? And what about CBS and ABC? How could they get all this done on $247? (Sometimes I think I worried too much as a child. It's worse now.)

All of this, of course, was before I came to understand the business of television. For example, when the host of a western series kept saying week after week that the show was being "brought to all you little cowboys and cowgirls" by the bakers of Silvercup Bread, I naturally assumed that the bakers, in addition to baking the bread, were involved in producing the show. I had visions of cameras and horses and cowboys trotting through this immense bakery, galloping among the ovens and sacks of flour, banging into bakers in tall white hats all amidst clouds of flour dust through which hurried freshly baked loaves of Silvercup Bread on conveyor belts headed in every direction and in all manner of confusion. (Remember, I was only seven.)

My older brother, on realizing my confusion, quickly disabused me of my ignorance by announcing to the world that I was an idiot. I was the only one in the room who didn't know the guys in the commercials (Ipana tooth paste, Fatima cigarettes, DeSoto automobiles) were paying the actors salaries and buying the hay for all the horses. Though humiliated before one and all, I did take some comfort in the knowledge that Howdy Doody wouldn't go off the air when the $247 ran out.

For most of us, television is our first and primary experience of shows, of drama. Through it we are introduced to created situations that model, with invented characters, human lives. Through television we first see human beings conceptualized, persons who do not exist per se, but characters who mold and affect the way we look at those who do.

In each of us, there is a capacity and a need for drama. We are, in our modern lives, relieved of the anxiety of starvation, of death from saber tooth tigers, of attack by bands of marauding Huns. But the instincts and drives by which our forebears survived these things remain in us still. They require exercise and expression, both of which can be found in drama.

Drama can thrill us with a dash across an ice flow through an arctic night, being stalked by a vicious animal in a darkened forest, or charging up a hill against an unseen enemy, all in the security of our home. Drama allows us the pleasure of a good cry when we are not sad, it keeps our emotions sharp when there is nothing in our daily lives to engage them. Magically, it can bring us to life when we do not feel alive and from this we can recharge ourselves, we can seek and reclaim our humanity.

We are, each of us, all of us. In each human being there is all of humanity, the limits of the knowing universe. At the same time, only a doubt's distance away, we can become alone, slip away from the whole. Drama can fix this. It is an art form that helps us find a fit and place in society. Drama done well goes to the very core of civilization — humanity reflecting on itself, human beings reflecting on their reason for being.

It is because good drama can be so beneficial to our emotional and spiritual health that we must guard against bad drama, a bad show. As for how bad a bad show can be, we need search no further than *Knots Landing,* an advertisement for which once heralded a new season with "...Twice the deceit! Twice the infidelity!" The attraction was not the cycle of drama, the sharing of angst, the testing of the human spirit, the triumph of hope. No. The attraction of *Knots Landing* that year was double portions of human beings failing, even refusing, to love.

Drama is a mechanism by which we communicate and seek to participate in the whole of humanity. It is because the need in us for drama is so important that we must judge whether a show is good or bad. You cannot sit before a bad show and not have your values dulled and your standards for living a good life lowered. You are wasting more than your time when you watch a bad show; you are lessening your potential to grow as a human being.

So be careful. That you can appreciate good drama is a measure of the miracle of human life. That you can be offered bad drama is a measure of how this miracle can be tarnished.

CORRUPTION

Read *The Godfather*
by Mario Puzo

‡ƆŊƠƦ

THERE WAS A MAN IN MY HOMETOWN whom I will call Ted, though that was not his real name. An engineer by training, he had taken a loan from an uncle and started a company. As Ted made his mark on commerce and community, he had married and bought a house on one of the nicer streets, near the bay. In time, his means dictated a larger house, so he built a two-story addition, one that was well received for its size and fit with the original structure.

After the passage of some years, Ted's mounting success called for a larger home in a more exclusive section of town. Now Ted was the son of a cousin of my father's and, being younger, he had known my father his entire life. Needing someone to close the sale of his house, he had asked my father to take care of it. However, as the papers for the closing made their way through the offices of real estate agents, tax registrars, law firms and guaranty companies, it was discovered that a permit to build the addition had never been issued.

The consequences of this could have been grave. Apart from the original fee not being paid, there were years of back taxes on the higher value of the house that had not been collected, plus fines and interest. More ominously, a law had been violated, the conviction of which would have sullied Ted's treasured reputation.

As it turned out, my father knew the person at the town hall responsible for issuing the proper clearances for the closing. Explaining that there must have been some oversight, he pleaded that the closing be allowed to proceed, if for no other reason than the buyers of the home had already sold their house and had no where else to live. In the end, reason prevailed, the papers were issued, and the sale closed with no fines or penalties paid or owing.

Now, my father was in practice with several other lawyers at the time and at a management meeting several months later it was noted that Ted had not paid his bill — the standard fee of $400. Being that Ted was a cousin of my father's and was well known to the others in the firm, my father suggested that it was an oversight and he would speak with Ted personally.

Well, he did speak to Ted — several times, in fact — and to no avail. More months passed and his fellow lawyers again asked about the bill and my father was left with little to say other that he would call again, which he did. In fact, he spoke with several people known to Ted to see if this was something personal or that he just didn't pay anyone. My father even talked to Ted's mother, a cousin with whom he had grown up. Again, to no avail.

The following spring, my father was at a family gathering — the christening of a newborn. Ted was also there, carrying himself with his full measure of confidence and industry. Moving through the gathering, nodding and speaking with cousins and cohorts, they came into one another's presence. I don't know how they started, but in time the issue of the $400 came up whereupon Ted reached for his money clip and said, "Look, Jack, I'm tired of this. How about I give you $200 cash and we call it even?" He held out two $100 bills with the wink of the worldly wise.

"You can keep your money," my father said, in disgust. "I'd rather be able to talk about you."

Honor is one of those qualities in people that is seen too often in the breach, in its absence. Ted was without honor. He held himself above the laws of the town and his obligation to a man he had known all his life, a man whose efforts had saved him many times the amount of the fee owed. Ted had engineered the theft of his own honor and then squandered the proceeds on his bank account.

Honor comes in different forms — verb, adjective, adverb and noun. We honor someone who has done well or done a good thing or lived a life we admire. A person is deemed honorable when they have served the community in some measurable fashion. A good man will act honorably — the adverb. Honor the noun, though, has another dimension. It has to do with something inside, with what we think about ourself. To understand this more completely, it is useful to consider whether it is possible to insult an honorable man, to insult a good man's honor.

After giving this some thought, I have come to the conclusion that it is not possible to do this. A man's honor is beyond insult. It is intact until he himself besmirches it or allows another man to affect it. To accept an insult as valid is to allow someone else to affect your honor when in fact your honor is your own creation, your own preserve.

A man's honor finds expression in the relationships he establishes with those around him. It is by the honor in each person that societies were built. It is by trust in others that we came to fill the moats of medieval castles and have built lives not on fear but on trust. It was this trust that Ted held in such contempt. Ted could not insult my father's honor, but by his offer he had tempted my father to do this to himself. And this was the violence of the act.

Had my father accepted the money, he would have participated in a theft, from his partners and himself. And had he responded with an obscenity or a show of anger, he would have left Ted with the satisfaction of having intruded on his peace of mind. To protect himself, my father refused to engage in the act or with the man. It was bad enough that Ted had stolen my father's good time. He was not about to let him affect his honor.

A person's honor should be sacred to him. It is his moral compass, the thing that he creates and that dictates what he can do and what he cannot do if he is to be the person he wills to be. Honor is not free, nor is it without consequence. To have honor is to accept the risk of being alone, the risk of having to disagree with others, even those whom you love.

This is not to say that in disagreement there is honor. It is to recognize that there are those around you who can be careless of their values and selfish of their needs who would have you act in a way that is inconsistent with your honor, with what you intend to be. You associate with such people at risk of becoming something other than yourself, at the risk of your honor.

Though honor is a private thing, it can find expression in the just pride we take in the things we have done and the things we have produced. In these we are saying to others, if not in so many words, "You can never really see inside of me and those things in me which I hold most dear, most sacred. But in this, this act I have done or this thing that I have made, it is in this that I invite you to see inside me as best you can for your own satisfaction and comfort."

This is as close as anyone should get to another person's honor.

CYNICS

Pity the Cynic
To mock truth and beauty
He first must recognize them
He sees truth and beauty and
Is afraid to engage them
He is a coward

MONEY

I AM AN ECONOMIST BY TRAINING, a profession second only to the law in the number of jokes told about those who practice it. There are comforts in being an economist, though, and first among these is that you can never be entirely wrong. There is always some way out, some assumption that can be changed or some theory that can be engaged to support your position, to explain every event and outcome *your* way. In truth, it's a contrarian's paradise.

Economics was dubbed the "dismal science" by the British social philosopher Thomas Carlisle, largely because of a 20+ year debate between two countrymen, Ricardo and Malthus, in the early 1800s. The debate was driven by Maltus' observation that any increase in economic production would only stimulate a growth in population that would soon consume the increased production — and more. In today's terms, it was a zero sum game in which the lower classes were condemned to a permanent state of subsistence, or less.

To be sure, things were not so great for the common man at that time, or for most of history. What Messrs Malthus and Carlisle had not counted on, though, were the likes of McCormick, Edison, Ford, Bell, Singer and Sloan, not to mention central banking, electronic communication and the emergence of political systems that, for all their faults, increasingly responded to the needs of the people they claimed to serve.

The key was increased productivity — more output from the same number of hours worked. It's done in two ways — technological development and capital accumulation — and it turned the United States from a nation of farmers to the greatest economic power in the history of the world, all in less than a century. By the mid-1950s, fewer than half the people working in the United States (i.e., less than a quarter of the population) produced what *all* the others consumed. And it continues. The Ford Motor Company built five cars for every production worker in 1992 against only three cars for every worker in 1978.

Of even greater importance to our growth was the vertical mobility of our human capital. While class distinctions and ethnic prejudices ran rampant, they were not insurmountable. Our most vital resource, human creativity, was not locked out of the process by reason of birth or caste. Someone with a good idea and the determination to bring it to market could reap the reward. Such people did not look at the world's resources as fixed, but as expanding — ideas yet to be had and developed. To them, the *status quo* was the other guy's problem.

And what does all this have to do with money? *Everything!* None of it happens, none of it works, literally, without money. Money, Money, Money. Preachers condemn it. Men kill for it. Women sleep for it. Loving couples fight over it. Children waste it. Grandparents hoard it. Monks disdain it. Bishops invest it. And we all need it.

In a money economy like our own, if you have money you can have anything that it can buy. A black man with money can send his child to a university at which his father could only wait tables and cook food. A farmhand can buy a correspondence course in computer science and move to the city as a technician. A city-bound stock broker can buy a farm on the Eastern Shore of Maryland to get away from the place where he earned the money with which he bought it. All this because of money, real MONEY. Money can free you from the physical and social trappings of your birth. If you got it, they gotta give you what they're selling — clothes, cars, homes, education...anything.

Paper money was created by the Chinese and brought to the West by Marco Polo. It had value because it could be redeemed in a precious metal — silver or gold — of a specified purity and weight. In reality, though, it was still barter. I give you 20 ounces of gold for so many cows and ducks or wagons and horses. Whether I give you the gold in kind or in paper redeemable in gold is a matter of mutual convenience, not substance. It is still so many things exchanged for so many other things. Gold and paper redeemable in gold were not "money" as we think of it today. They were still just things.

But, over time, paper money secured and redeemable in gold or silver allowed more than one person to use the same brick of gold, the same stored value. It allowed for the creation of banking as we know it today. A banker's certificate for 20 ounces of gold redeemable in 90 days time meant that the banker could let someone else use the value of the 20 ounces for 89 days. The result was that at least three people had the benefit of the same brick of gold — the person holding the paper (the depositor), the person to whom the bank had lent it and, of course, the bank, which collected interest from the person to whom it had lent the brick. This was the beginning of money. But it was still one step away from modern money because it was still built on redeemability in a precious metal.

During the Depression, President Franklin Roosevelt made it illegal for individuals to hold gold — other than in jewelry and such things. Gold's value was fixed by law at $35 the ounce. That was the rate at which the U.S. Federal Reserve would redeem dollar denominated obligations held by foreigners. Regularly we would read stories in the newspapers and business weeklies about our trade deficit and dollars flowing out as measured by gold moving around in the basement of the New York Federal Reserve Bank, from one country's bin to the next, moving out of the US bin into Japan's or Germany's or some other country's bin.

As the world economy continued to surge through the post war boom, our imports from Europe and Japan far outstripped exports. The gold was flowing out of our bins in the Fed so fast that President Nixon suspended convertibility of the dollar in August 1971. In effect, he was saying to the rest of the world: "You got dollars? Buy American! We're keeping the gold for ourselves!" The earth shook — but the world had no alternative. It was in no one's interest to collapse the value of the dollar. Everything was denominated in it, most specifically U. S.

Treasury bonds that were held by princes, presidents and poor people's retirement funds around the globe. We had written so much paper that the world could not afford to cash it in. Our debt, in effect, had become the world's store of value, its currency.

This is money as we use it today. Take a dollar out of your pocket. Look it over. It is a Federal Reserve Note. Period. Its value derives from the fact that our laws require a person offering something for sale to take a Federal Reserve Note in payment. Ask a banker about it; i.e., what, exactly, a dollar is. There are few who will be able to give you a really satisfactory answer. In fact, maybe you shouldn't ask.

Our currency is not backed by gold, as many still suppose, but by our legal and political system, by our mutual faith in that system and in one another — as a country and as a people. A dollar has value because we have collectively agreed, as an act of faith in one another, to accept it in all transactions public and private. That's it. That's all there is. What stands behind the dollar is ourselves and the faith we invest in the political system under which we live. We give it value. At the end of the day, *we* are its value.

And it is because of our mutual faith in one another that we can use money to store and convey our most precious commodity — time. Money can store time's value from one year to the next. It can move the value of accumulated time among cities, across continents and oceans and between countries of diametrically opposed political systems. Time's value can be assembled in dollar amounts and moved about in money. Money can efficiently transfer surpluses to places and situations that create still greater surpluses. It is the medium of growth.

Even more, money allows us each and individually to accommodate the most pressing and unremitting force in history — change. The world is in constant change. Because of money, we can change with it. We can sell our land and invest in corporate bonds, or we can sell our bonds and buy a house in another city where there's more work and, when we are finished working, we can sell our house and buy an annuity on which to live in retirement. Money allows us to transfer value across change, from the old to the new, across time.

If we are daring and clever (and lucky!), we can use

money to lead change and accumulate still more money, vast amounts of it. We can have so much of it that we literally don't know what to do with it, so much that it would seem to separate us from the touchstones of mortal life — the constraints of time, the need for food, the fear of bodily harm, of the world around us in general. Some people with this much money fall prey to seeing themselves as superhuman, god-like creatures, Masters of the Universe, who, if not all powerful, are certainly less answerable to the laws of nature and conscious than lesser beings. And this is the turn, the place where it can all go wrong.

Because money is time in so many ways, having a great amount of it can separate us from time's value. Too much of it can suspend time and thus remove from our lives the links to the physical imperatives of the world about us, from our individual mortality. And to live a life that ignores, or would deny, our mortality, is to live beneath the truth — it is to live a lie.

And there's more. Having a great deal of money can lead a person to see all of his responsibilities in terms of it. It can tempt a parent to see his duties as being met if he meets his children's worldly needs — food and shelter, clothing and education — in great abundance and with a flourish. In effect, the financially independent can become totally dependent on finances, and this can make being a human being — a caring, engaged and spiritually developing person — more difficult.

So be careful about money. Too much of it *can* hurt you.

These risks aside, though, money is one of the great liberating vehicles of the modern era. It works not because of avarice and greed, but because of the rule of law and our mutual faith in one another. We cannot live without it anymore than we can live without food and shelter. It is how we get these things. It is essential to the processes by which these things come to be made. Though romantics and radicals may rail against it, money is a necessary good and anyone who tries to tell you that it is not important just isn't paying attention.

WISDOM

Nothing in life is free
Not friends, not freedom
Not laughter, not love
Not faith, not courage
Not discipline, not patience
Not knowledge, not wisdom
Least of all wisdom
Not the getting of it
Not the having of it

LEARNING

IT WOULD NOT BE INACCURATE TO SAY that what I took from my four years at Boston College was more absorbed than learned. As with many of my classmates of those prosperous years, 1961-1965, the operative variables in the decision for me to go to college in the first place were that I had the time and my parents had the money.

Other forces, of course, were at play, not the least of these being a rigorous process of tribal selection by which the better jobs and the prettier girls went to the guys in the button down shirts, the guys with the college degrees. It was they who had learned how to learn. It was they who were coming to an understanding of the needs and structures that would drive the post-industrial state.

While some thrived academically in this environment, I did not. The intake of knowledge as quantifiably measured on my transcript could be most charitably characterized as undistinguished. This is not to say that I did not enjoy my years at The Heights. I did very much and I can't remember knowing anyone who did not. It is to say, though, that I was perhaps not yet fully engaged in the process of higher learning — either for life or from it.

There were moments, though, when the clouds of youth that surrounded my still training mind were not so dense as to block out *all* knowledge and learning. And, in truth, there were quite a few such moments. Perhaps my real difficulty was in connecting them. Be that as it may, one such moment occurred on an afternoon in the spring of my senior year. In an instant I caught a passing glimpse of what I had been missing, a moment from an unexpected corner and one which I carry with me to this day.

It was April, warm and bright. The class was Fr. Harney's. The subject was History. Before going on, I should note that Fr. Harney was not young, perhaps in his mid-sixties. As for stature, well, there wasn't much of him, maybe five foot three inches, with a professor's full paunch. Cursed with poor eyesight, he wore thick glasses that magnified his eyes and gave him a comical appearance. A Jesuit of the old school, he was clever enough to know what was going on, or, better put, what was not going on. We were not there to learn History or anything else. We were there to get the required course work done and to move on.

"The Lives of the Saints" was how we referred to Fr. Harney's course. Now there should be no mistaking the fact that Fr. Harney would never pass up an opportunity to note where a saint was born or beheaded. However, the primary reason for the Lives of the Saints appellation was his fixation on the great cathedrals of Europe, renderings of which he displayed with great pride and care along the north wall of the room on the first floor of Fulton Hall.

Anyway, as I said, it was an April afternoon, perhaps only four weeks — twelve classes! — from the end of it all, from graduation and the world beyond, from the start of our own histories. It was the first class after lunch and what might best be described as the pack of us had seated ourselves before Fr. Harney's lectern, the warmth of the Boston spring full in our lungs and minds. As I think back on it, we might have been forgiven, at least on such an afternoon, for not training our minds on the subject of the day's lecture — Europe between the wars.

Now WWII and the events leading up to it were subjects in which I had had an abiding interest since high school and for this reason I was following the lecture more closely than normal. I could sense Fr. Harney's frustration at the lack of attention from the others in the room, though, and I found myself feeling sorry for him. Here was an old man struggling to teach us what he thought was important, an old man, perhaps, just struggling to teach. After a few moments, he paused, closed his notebook and began to tell about an experience he had had as a student in Europe during the twenties. It went something like this:

"I was with two friends," he began. "One was an older American Jesuit and the other a German student. The student had been telling us about a veteran of the Great War who had started a new political party and would be speaking at a nearby beer garden that evening. He invited us to come, which we were happy to do.

"Well, of course, it was Hitler, and in no time at all the man had those before him in a frenzy, screaming about the Jews taking over one half the world and the communists and Slavs taking over the other half. Before it was over, they were ready to break out into the streets and start brawling and they might have done so if the police hadn't shown up and kept them inside until the fever had passed.

"In listening to Hitler, I must confess to a certain excitement at first. But this passed as the hate in man's soul spilled out in every thing he said. As we were walking back to the University, I asked the German student what he thought about Hitler, about his prospects. 'Blah!' the student said shrugging. 'Hitler is nothing — a harmless fool with the gift of oratory.'

"On hearing this, the Jesuit, who had been silent since we had left the beer garden, turned to the student and said, 'Know this, my son. No fool with the gift of oratory is harmless.'

"Now," Harney said, his voice rising, his face flushed, "if that doesn't mean anything to you, if that doesn't tell you to wake up and listen to what there is to learn, then there's no hope!"

The room went still. From his tone, those who had not been listening sensed that they had missed something. Of course, there were the odd guffaws — the final defense of the hopelessly ignorant. And a few asked those about them what had happened, what it was that Fr. Harney had said. But the moment had passed, unabsorbed. Fr. Harney went back to his notebook, the others to whatever it was they were thinking about.

After graduation, I spent a year in Baghdad with the Jesuits' Lay Apostolate program. On the way, I had visited the cathedral at Rheims. It was late on an August afternoon—bright

69

and clear and dry. As my companion and I searched for a parking place, it was impossible not to be struck by the sheer size of the building, seeming to have shot up as some great outcropping of rock, its thousands of stones and statues like fissures and cracks in what might have been the top of a great Alpine mountain just below the surface of the earth.

As we entered the portal, I remembered what Fr. Harney had told us about the time it had taken to build such things — eighty to one hundred years — and that no man who had begun to build one had ever lived to see it done or had any hope of it. These cathedrals were something more than places to pray, Fr. Harney had told us, they were prayers in themselves, the expressions and acts of mortal man seeking something beyond his own life—the immortal.

After returning from Baghdad, I spent the summer of 1966 at Boston College taking economics courses to begin work on a graduate degree. Living in the dorms of the upper campus, I made a practice of walking at night before going to bed. One night, between Bapbst Library and St. Mary's Hall, a portly figure approached, its stride rocking slightly as an older person might do to favor a hip or sore knee. It was Fr. Harney.

That he didn't recognize me was hardly surprising. Undaunted, I introduced myself and told him about my year in Baghdad and about seeing the cathedral at Rheims and, on my way home, Notre Dame in Paris, and that I now understood some of the things he was trying to tell us. He spoke briefly about the frustration of teaching, but his tone was hopeful, that he understood that people would learn things if you didn't give up, if you told them enough times. I shook his hand and we went our separate ways, he to St. Mary's and I to the dorms.

I never saw Fr. Harney again — but I did read about him. It was in Paris in 1976 or 1977. I was on a U. S. Government delegation for the Treasury Department and my link back to home was the Paris Herald Tribune. Looking through it one night, my eye caught Fr. Harney's name. It was his obituary. In it I read that he had been a distinguished scholar, and had been recognized as such in Europe and the United States. The classes came back to me — the pack putting in the hours, waiting to get out, missing what was there. Then there was the memory of his experience of Hitler in the beer garden and, finally, seeing him on campus that summer night.

As I studied the three paragraphs in the obituary, I sensed a balance to it all. For me, to see what he was saying, to know and understand the past, to see that our first duty as citizens of the future is to avoid the mistakes of those who have gone before us. And then the final measure of the balance scale, the final justice for the man who understood history, for the professor of the "Lives of the Saints," — an obituary in the Paris Herald Tribune. His just due.

We should all live to enjoy such success — to know as much and to learn as well as Fr. Harney. God bless and keep him.

HELP

If you have not helped someone to be better
You have done nothing

JOBS

I AM NOW FIFTY-TWO YEARS OLD and there's not a man in my generation who doesn't know that, in the old west, they hung a horse thief. The demise of the western, which so filled the movie houses and TV screens of my youth, may have left succeeding generations ignorant of this. And even among the informed, there may not be a complete understanding for the severity of the punishment. The reason is simple; stealing a man's horse in the middle of the Dakota Territory was the same as killing him.

First among the western heroes of my childhood was Hoppalong Cassidy. "Hoppy," to his devoted fans, over-whelmed the youth of the early 1950s as millions sat glued to black and white screens in their living rooms. (Family rooms came later.) Though introduced to TV fans in the 1950s, the films were actually made in the 1930s, complete with Gabby Hayes, the toothless wonder who gave us "jumpingeehossafats" and perhaps even "dern tootin."

As any Hoppy fan will remember, there was no skimping on the production costs. In a Hoppalong Cassidy episode, a posse was a small army of 100 or more horsemen storming across the range at a speed and force that made your blood race. Given that the old west closed after the turn of the century, it seems plausible that several of the extras in the series had witnessed a horse thief or two being hung. It is certain that any number of them had worked the open range and had a per-sonal understanding of a world where to lose your horse was to confront death from exposure and starvation.

By any measure, the old west is a distant place to us

today living at the dawn of the third millennium. Even the 1930's may seem remote, a time when a twenty-two pound mechanical calculator built on a cast iron frame was a state of the art office machine. But it was not really that long ago. An eighty year old man today would have been twenty in the middle of the Great Depression. And we forget too easily that during the 1930s people starved to death in this country, and millions more who had once been well fed went to bed hungry every night. In the pit of the Great Depression, a job could be the difference between living and dying; during the Great Depression, a man's horse was his job.

By the 1950s, all this had changed. With the GI Bill and a world rebounding from the ravages of war and exploding in growth from the technology spawned by it, opportunities abounded. Couples who in the depth of the Depression would have been happy to see their grown children land a job in the mill, were now parents of lawyers, doctors, and vice presidents of great corporations who drove fancy cars and belonged to country clubs. Jobs had become careers and careers had become lives and lifestyles.

At the core of all of this, though, was still a basic operative; you worked to get money for food and shelter. Of what was left, you saved most, and occasionally splurged on a night out with the rest. Prosperity and having a good time on a regular basis took some getting used to for a generation that had spent a decade in depression and four years at war. By the late 1950s, though, things had been good for some time and looked to be getting even better. What could possibly be wrong with working your way up the corporate ladder at IBM with a second car in the driveway, stock options at below market and money in the bank?

A lot, it would seem. The 1960s began under a new president, a man who had never wanted for anything in his life. For him, the basics — food and shelter — were never in doubt. He saw a country with its belly full and its feet dry, and turned its attention to more important things — its sins. There were rights to be guaranteed, wrongs to be righted. Poverty was to be stamped out, new frontiers to be found. The torch had indeed been passed to a new generation of Americans. Our campaign to land a man on the moon and return him safely to earth was to be launched "not because it is easy, but because it is hard."

Well, Americans had been doing hard things for some time. The pioneers who settled the West *walked* there, some from St. Louis all the way to California. Veterans of World War II had done a lot of "hard" things, as well. They walked several hundred yards in waste deep water in full battle dress while Germans or Japanese were shooting real bullets at them. They had done these hard things not because they wanted to, but because they didn't see any alternative. Doing things that were hard "because they were hard," though, that was a little different look.

We were challenged to ask not what our country could do for us, but we could do for our country. Plain ol' doing something for ourselves and those closest and dearest to us did not appear to be a meaningful option. It wasn't enough to have a job, now we had to make a contribution. Each one of us had to make a difference. It was the dawn of the modern age of causes, of the collectivization of our individual aspirations.

A-type executives, the knights of the post-war boom, the guys who put it together and made it all work, were debased. Astronauts, athletes and activists were the new currency, the new heroes, though none of them ever really made anything or caused anything to be made. And conspicuous consumption — the way a man demonstrated his productivity in a world where few really knew or cared what he did for a living — was reviled. In the land of plenty, sack cloth, self-denial and suffering were the order of the day.

In this age of causes, you didn't have a hair on your socially conscious ass if you didn't give up two years of your life to join the Peace Corps, learn Urdu and teach unemployed Pakistanis how to play basketball. Abbeys and convents across the land soon emptied as government funded programs in every state and city allowed young men and women to make a difference without having to wear a collar or a habit.

None of this is to say that the Peace Corps was not a good idea nor a useful place to spend two years. Nor is to say that JFK's New Frontier and LBJ's Great Society were unworthy or did not meet real needs. It is to say that in this period we began to ask too much of our jobs, our professions. We not only wanted our jobs to provide us with food and shelter, we wanted them to provide personal fulfillment, something they could promote, but not completely achieve. We had secularized our emotional, religious and spiritual needs and packed them all into our ten hour a day jobs — and then began wondering what happened to our personal, private lives.

I am an executive recruiter. Regularly I meet executives who see their lives as increasingly devoid of meaning, especially those who see their prospects for further professional advancement limited. Typically, they have devoted their lives to their work and now see their work as running out on them, failing them. For many of these, their problem is not with their work, but with what their work means to them. They have let it become the primary measure of their worth and source of fulfillment.

The disappointment of such executives should not be surprising. We are encouraged from childhood to challenge ourselves to do more, to score higher, to compete with those around us. Well, there comes a time when this loses its usefulness, even becomes destructive. If you are doing good work that is well regarded by your peers, serves some useful purpose and provides you with the wherewithal to meet your responsibilities, then things aren't really all that bad.

Accepting this as success is not easy for many pushed since childhood by parents, teachers and coaches to do more, to make a difference. But the time must come when your achievements meet your potential, when you have gone as far as you can go with what you have. And when this does finally happen, the solution is not in finding a new job, but in finding more in the life you already have. It is certainly not in wanting more from your work, your job, than it can provide.

Fulfillment is a balance between your needs and what you are realistically able to do about them. It means doing a job that can be managed on a normal day at less than 110 percent. It means that your children are growing up with good values, have good friendships and enjoy your company. It means that you and your spouse are growing together, not apart. It means that your world is not getting bigger, but you know it better and enjoy it more.

At the end of the day, we can, each of us, do things of value, be useful to ourselves and to those about us. The trick in life is finding out what these things are. The victory in life is in having these things be enough.

GLORY

Seek Courage
Never Glory

COUNTRY

I WAS BORN IN 1943, A CITIZEN OF THE UNITED STATES. I am also an American. Exactly when this happened, I cannot be certain. In fact, it may still be happening.

The world was at war in 1943. German armies roamed the Caucuses and paraded in the streets of Paris and Brussels. Japanese soldiers strolled the avenues of Saigon and Manila, Hong Kong and Shanghai. The future of liberal democracy, the notion that governments exist to serve the governed, hung in the balance — literally and in fact.

It was a time when the sun never set on the killing. A day begun in a Nazi concentration camp in Poland would pass over Allied bombings in Germany, U-boats sinking American tankers off the Delaware coast, Japanese soldiers killing Eskimos in the Aleutians, Americans bombing Japanese positions in Guadalcanal, Japanese killing Chinese partisans outside Beijing, Gurkhas killing Japanese in Burma and end with Germans and Russians dying by the thousands at Stalingrad. If we didn't have film of it all, if we couldn't document the more than 50 million who died in it, if we didn't have millions still living with the scars, the stumps and the tattoos, it would be hard to believe that it actually happened. But it did.

For all the horror and destruction of it, though, World War II had been a just war. The aggressor states had been defeated. The good guys had won...well, mostly. Of the five principal belligerents, three were autocracies (Germany, Japan, the USSR) and two were democracies (Britain and the United States.) Both of the democracies were on the winning side, as was one of the autocracies, the USSR. However, with the common enemy of Germany defeated, the incompatibility of the Soviet political system — Communism — with that of its democratic allies soon became manifest.

Allies no longer, the democracies and the USSR maneuvered for position and power and, as with the war just won, the principal field of contest was Europe. This place from which our core political values had sprung now lay in ruin, its farms and factories in disarray, unable to feed and clothe its peoples. Once proud states were on the brink of chaos, easy pickings for a victorious Soviet Union which boasted the largest standing army in the history of the world. All that had been won back from one autocracy was at risk of slipping away to another.

A hero was needed.

For much of the war, Harry Truman had been a second tier U. S. Senator from Missouri, a man known to few outside his home state. Decorated for bravery in World War I, he had been thrust into national office as Franklin Roosevelt's running mate in 1944, succeeding to the presidency on Roosevelt's death in April 1945. A student of history, Truman understood that winning the peace was going to be as important as winning the war. More importantly, he had the courage to act on what he knew.

In what Churchill termed "the most unsordid act in history," the Truman Administration provided sixteen billion dollars in aid to Europe under the Marshall Plan — a staggering sum in those years. With this money, Truman bought time for the democratic and economic structures of pre-war Europe to recover. The Europe we have today, where 350 million people live in peace and prosperity, could not have been achieved without it.

Less obvious than the success of the Marshall Plan was the premise on which it was undertaken. The premise was that man is not only born with certain inalienable rights, but that man is born good and that good men, if allowed, will seek compatibility, not hostility. More precisely, a world of governments made by, for and of good men would be disinclined toward war.

This was the premise. It would remain the hope in an extended contest of influence and nerves between the United

States and the Soviet Union, a contest that not one of the world's leaders at the end of World War II would live to see resolved. Ridding the world of Hitler had taken six years. The fall of the Soviet Union, of Stalin and his legacy, would require another forty-five.

Of Nazi Germany and the Soviet Union, honest men can differ as to which was worse. While saying anything but evil about Nazi Germany is hazardous, it can be said that, for all its sins, it never claimed to be good — only right by birth and might. Nazism prayed on the worst in man, on his avarice and greed, on his fear. It was evil incarnate, a virus of the human condition that was righteously abhorred and beneficially destroyed.

The Soviet Union, though, was even more insidious and this because it was built on a system that prayed not on the worst in man, but on the best. It exploited his compassion and sense of fair play. This was the enemy now, hidden not among the street toughs of Munich's beer halls, but among those who would serve their fellow man and make a better world.

Though embraced by many in the intellectual community, communism was little more than materialism raised to a state religion. On birth and from it, a person was a ward of a state from which all things came and to which all things belonged. By this new religion, people were not to be equal before the law, but the *same* — it was the world of the average. Those who were less than average were condemned as slackers. Those who were better than average were condemned as elitists.

The premise of this system was not that man was good, but that he was bad, that in him was an evil that only the state could be trusted to purge. In this system, a man was not to be trusted with coming to his own judgments or with seeking a spiritual dimension to his life. In this system, man was to be controlled in these urges for the betterment of the state. And make no mistake — this mistrust of man's nature and the ritual crushing of individual initiative that ensued was not an aberration of this system, but its core belief and purpose. It was what they meant to do.

Of all the trademarks of the Soviet Union, none is more telling than the ordinariness of its ruling class. Other great powers had been built by dynamic leaders who had forged their will on the energy of the people. Not so the Soviet Union. It was built by bureaucrats who were threatened by creativity and crushed it at every opportunity. It was a dictatorship of the mediocre to whom the creation of a state had become the objective in itself.

And so as the world passed from war to peace, the countries of the world settled into one of three camps: countries based on the premise that man was good; countries based on the premise that man was not good; and countries that did not have the luxury of time or resource to focus on either proposition. What ensued was a conflict in which the first two camps built arsenals that no sane person could imagine employing and sought justification by imitation among the countries in the third camp.

This was the Cold War. It was a war not so much of tanks and territory, but of ideas and beliefs. It was a time when uniforms were worn on the inside, when it was hard to tell which side someone might be on, so every word was weighed, every inflection scrutinized. It was a time when those espousing freedom would deny its expression to those they suspected of abusing it. It was a time when the disenfranchised at home were shouted down for the audacity to seek equality before the law. It was a time when those seeking justice overseas were played against one another in the name of freedom. It was a time when we slept with whores in the name of fidelity and family.

But throughout this war, the premise held: Man is good and he can be trusted to do good things. It was the core of our strength, our most powerful weapon. As others invaded us with their deceits, we pushed on in the knowledge that among our enemies were our allies, that in the states aligned against us, there lived people who were good and were inclined to do good things.

History is a tale of nations in conflict, of empires rising and falling — Egypt, Greece, Rome, China, Germany, Spain, Japan, Portugal, France, Britain, and the USSR. Strength and growth, security and wealth. These were sought and found as nations spread out from their borders and settled or conquered new lands. World War II was the death knell of the French and British empires. And the Soviet Empire is now gone as well, buried in the rubble and dust of a wall in Berlin, it torn down by the people it had imprisoned. The world is now, by and large, rid of empire. Think of it.

None of this is to say that the United States is without fault, nor that mistakes were not made nor people hurt. It is to say that in the history of the world there has not been a larger portion of its peoples living under governments which are by law and practice responsive to the needs of their citizens. It is to say that not since the Dark Ages, literally, has Europe been free of a major war for as long. It is to say that war as a means of resolution among the major powers of the earth is not now a viable option. Think about *that*.

Much of this is because of what the United States did after World War II. And much of what we did was no more than the continuing evolution of our national character, one unique in the history of the world. A breed of human being that any human being can become. A breed that excludes none and can include all. A breed built not on caste nor race, but on choice and will. A breed whose best days will always lie before it, a breed whose greatest treasure is its faith in the future. A breed called *American*.

And if you want to know when to start worrying about your country, about America, listen for a silence. If this country is ever to die, its decline will be marked from the day the Americans living in it stopped speaking up — from the day they stopped trying to make it better.

It *is* still happening.

LIVING

In living we search on
Driven by unknown truths whose
Discovery and learning we come to
More by faith than knowledge

RELIGION

THE FIRST TIME I CAN REMEMBER being in church was with my mother. It was a chilly afternoon, probably during Lent. She had gone in for a "visit," which people were encouraged to do back then. I was four years old and had been pestering her to take me with her. The hard wood pews, however, combined with the darkness of the place and the absence of anything to hold my attention for more than five complete seconds created a critical need in me to move about, to squirm on the seat of the pew to the disturbance of the quiet of the place. After several remonstrations and strong grippings of the upper arm, my mother, distracted from prayer, brought me up close — eye to eye — and in a strong, threatening whisper said, "Do you ever want me to bring you to church again?"

"No," I replied.

My mother would laugh deeply each time she told that story. She liked the directness of my answer, the truth of it. And beyond these, it was a story she was telling on herself. The experience had taught her the folly of expecting a young boy only recently in full control of his bodily functions to have any hope of understanding what was going on in a church.

For most of us, our first introduction to and earliest experiences of religion are forced. Children do not spontaneously rise on a Sunday morning and troop off to church. Why would any child want to go to a place where he will have to sit quietly and still for an hour? Religion is just not by instinct a kid's thing.

Religion is, however, a very human thing. Love and war

aside, nothing is more common in the human experience. Few are the recorded cultures that have banned religion, and none of consequence has endured, the USSR being the most recent to go. In our modern world, religion is a structure that runs parallel to the civil order, something to meet the needs that the temporal structure cannot fulfill.

The presence of religion in virtually every culture and in virtually every recorded century points to the need in man for a spiritual experience. (In this sense, certainly, spirituality is reality.) In practicing a religion, we are taking our bodies and minds to a place and time where our souls can engage and grow. Religion provides a rhythm in our temporal lives in which our spiritual lives can find expression.

As children, we are taught prayers by rote and, further, that the repetition of these prayers is praying. But praying must be more than repeating words, more than a chant. Praying is listening, as well, searching for the inner voice resting within each of us that speaks only when we listen for it. And it is in hearing that voice that we become aware of the bit of God living within each of us.

Too often religion is fear-driven. People turn to their religious structures for support when they are afraid of failure, or harm, or loss, or death. There are also those who dwell on fearing God, who seem glad to embrace a God of retribution and vengeance. I will never understand this. There is fear enough in a life without looking to God for more.

Religion also can dwell too much on death and what lies beyond it. A life lived by rules set from afar to avoid an eternity of punishment is a life spent in fear. A religion that exploits our fear of death to keep us in the fold is not worthy of our practice. A religion must first be for the living, for a meaning to life as we are living it. This is not to say that a religion should not have rules. It is to say that before rules, a religion must have values and if a religion's rules get in the way of its values, then the rules must be changed, or the religion be abandoned.

It has been largely in the practice of religion that man has focused on those needs that exist beyond his stomach and groin. It is through religion that he has sought to reach his potential to live a better life, one that embraces his spiritual needs, those that burrow deep inside each one of us and, when found, free us from time and place. Failing to recognize the role religion has played in the development of our values hampers our ability to protect and enhance them and lessens our appreciation of the need to pass them on to those who follow.

Ultimately, the purpose of any religion must be to promote a spiritual dimension in our lives. A religion should not be measured so much by the charitable works it performs, but by whether it challenges us to find a meaning in life beyond the temporal world. The spirit that lives inside each of us — the bit of God — seeks expression and growth. And this is what a religion should do — encourage and help us to nurture this spirit, this soul, so that it will grow within us, so that we can be more than what we eat and own.

To deny yourself a religion is to take life's most challenging journey — the exploration and discovery of the spiritual potential of your life — alone, without the help of those who are with you now and those who have gone before. So be good to yourself. Go to a church, sit quietly and still — and listen.

DOUBT

Doubt is an opportunity to believe
A near occasion of faith

DEPENDENCY

THERE IS THE STORY ABOUT THE BOY who did not speak. In all other respects he was normal. He could read and write, and seemed to enjoy doing each. They knew that he could hear because he responded to sound and understood what others said to him and generally did what he was told. Though he never laughed out loud, he smiled broadly when amused, nodding his head, sometimes vigorously, occasionally even slapping his knee.

His mother had tried to hide her concern. "He'll speak," she would say to relatives and neighbors. "He's a good boy...never a minute's trouble." Inside, of course, she was heartbroken. Here was her only child from her husband dead now five years, unable to speak, unable to tell her what he needed.

When the boy was just a year old, she took him to a specialist to see what could be done. The doctor had asked her if the boy had ever made what appeared to be voluntary sounds. She had said yes, but in her despair over the loss of her husband whom she had loved dearly, she could not honestly remember whether the boy had ever made a controlled sound. Despite all the tests and diagnoses, no solution could be found. There was nothing to be done.

In time, she and the boy had settled into a rhythm of life, she at work, he at pre-school and kindergarten, then first grade. In some ways, the boy's not speaking became a bond between them, a shared burden that set them apart from the outside world. Relatives and friends came to accept them — the widow and her

97

boy who did not speak. In fact, they came to be admired for their closeness and the success each secured in life, she as the assistant librarian and he as an "A" student in first grade where he had been excused from all oral requirements of class participation.

During the winter the boy turned seven, a niece of his mother's was to be married. Relatives came from all around. Staying in the boy's house was Cousin Robert, a large man with opinions to match. Cousin Robert was assigned the convertible sofa in the basement. His calling was the management of an appliance store in a town some seventy miles distant where he also served on the board at the hospital. Never married, he found his company in that of other men, most of whom found their company away from their wives and children. Cousin Robert had distinguished himself in several respects, but none more remarkably than in the fact that he had never once in his entire life been wrong, about *anything*.

Cousin Robert's concern for the boy had been early and apparent, enquiring about the boy whenever he called, whether he had started to talk or what else was wrong with him. On this morning, Cousin Robert was coming to the breakfast table where the boy already sat. "Move back there, will you, boy," he said. "Make room for Cousin Robert." With this, Cousin Robert pushed the table away from the wall so that his considerable girth could fit between it and the table with sufficient arm and shoulder room to get at his food.

Now seated, he looked at the boy's mother who was fixing breakfast. His appetite was whetted by the aroma of sausage and frying eggs and warming cinnamon buns. He looked at the boy who sat silently, looking straight ahead. "Boy..." he said, waiting until the boy had turned toward him. "Boy," he continued, "I read in the paper the other week about kids these days and what's wrong with them." He paused again, looking out of the corner of his eye to see if the boy's mother was listening. Satisfied that she was, he continued.

"Kids are all screwed up in this country, understand? Drugs, broken homes, fathers running all over. Article said that the leading cause of death in male teenagers was death by gun shot. Gunned down. Out in front of their homes, in schools, just about anywhere." He winked at the boy, made his hand into a gun, brought his thumb down like the hammer of pistol. "Pop!" he said. "You dead." He took a sip of his coffee, his eyes fixing on the boy. "Maybe you better off not talking, boy. Keep your mouth shut, you stay out of trouble...won't get shot." Cousin Robert liked this, a lot. He laughed to himself. "See, boy," he said, "there's good in everything, you just got to look for it."

Cousin Robert took another sip of his coffee and looked toward the boy's mother. "Why they having this reception at the lodge and not over to that big room at the hotel? Hotel's a lot nicer. Better food, cleaner. Looks like something. Guess it costs more, but hell, they only got but the one daughter. What would it be? Another $1,000? That George, he always was the tight one. Some times he squeaked." He made a squeaking sound in his throat as he looked at the boy and laughed.

The boy's mother brought over the breakfast plates and set them before her son and Cousin Robert.

"Don't understand this President Clinton," Cousin Robert started. "Read the other day "

She smiled at the boy, moving the butter nearer his reach. The boy turned from Cousin Robert, who continued to speak, up to his mother. She looked at him and froze...she could see that he wanted to say something. The muscles in his cheeks quivered as his mouth began to open, halting at first and then working as if to form a word. Still frozen, she was afraid even to hope what might happen. The boy put his head down, as if swallowing, and as he raised his head, the word "Mama" blurted out, first low and then again, louder. "M-Mama."

"Yes, son. Oh, yes!" she said, bringing her hands to her face. "I'm your mama!" She'd lost her breath and could not move. Tears welled in her eyes.

"Mama," the boy repeated.

"Yes, son."

"Mama, is this asshole ever gonna shut up?"

"What'd that boy say?"

"Shut up, Robert," she said as she sat down next to the boy, grasping his shoulder and arm. "Johnny! For God's sake, child, you can talk!"

"Yes," said the boy. "I've always been able to talk."

"Then why didn't you? I mean, all these years, all the doctors, all the tests. Why didn't you ever say anything?"

"Well," the boy said, looking at Cousin Robert, "up till now, things have been pretty good."

In the end, and from the beginning, we are all dependent. It is the natural state. The only real questions are On what? On whom? and By how much? Cheated by fate of the company of a father, wounded by the sorrow of his mother, the boy had assumed a handicap and by this shifted his burden to those around him. Cousin Robert, however, had made the handicap more burden to the boy than relief, so he gave it up. Turns out, there is some good in everything.

There is, inside each of us, a struggle between the part of us that wants to be completely independent and the part that knows that this is impossible. Though we instinctively see this struggle as one of independence, it is more usefully seen as one over those things on which we are to be dependent. Ultimately, it is a struggle over how much we choose to develop our abilities and how much we choose to control our needs. It is about discipline.

When we are young, the desire to be independent comes in rushes. Growing and seeking its form, the person inside of us bangs against the things around it — parents and rules, friends and structures. Amidst silent and not so silent screams, another whole birthing is done. And though aided by the midwifery of family and friends, this birthing must ultimately be done alone, and much of it in empty places filled with people we have only met and do not know. It is a passage from which no one is safe.

Within this chaos, our measurable steps from complete dependency are small ones. Doing chores for money so we don't have to ask for it. Taking care of the things we have so that we won't need anyone else's. Freeing our self from those who teach us by learning what they know. And yet with each step we take toward independence, we form new links with new people and new things on whom and on which we develop new dependencies.

To be completely independent is to be completely

separate from society. Complete independence means to act without regard to the impact our actions have on other people. But, at its core, this is unhuman because to be human is to act in the cognizance of the consequence of our actions. Complete independence means an isolation so complete as to deny existence as a human being. It is, in fact, an impossible state for a sane person.

For my part, I do not wish to live a life removed from other people, an idle hermit whose function and achievement is the taking of nourishment from fruits and berries to sustain a life spent alone, unchallenged, and then given up silently in some distant glen. I have married. I have fathered and raised children. I am not only part of humanity, I have had a hand in its continuance, in its future creation, in what and where it will be after I am no longer in it. Though dependent throughout life, it is my hope that those on whom I have been dependent have been dependent on me as well, that our shared dependencies have enhanced and mutually enriched our lives.

Of the things you will learn as you grow, nothing is more important to learn than that you are dependent. That which endures and fulfills, that which sustains and strengthens, that which provides the balance you need to grow as a person and as a spiritual being, is a close and deep understanding of your dependencies.

Choose them carefully.

TROUBLES

Don't be too hard on your troubles
They help to define the life you are leading
Besides, you could have someone else's

KEYS

NOTHING MORE SEPARATES MAN from the other creatures of the earth than his free will. By it he chooses to lead or to follow, to challenge or to accept, to build or to destroy, to serve or to be served, to be what he wants to be or to be what others see him as. Because man has a will, he can understand that the value of a thing is not in the having of it, but in how it was come by. It is because man has a will, because he can choose to affect things, that he can live beyond the physical world into which he was born.

But nothing is without cost, and so it is with free will. It is by free will that man becomes imperfect, can make a mistake, by which he is introduced to the reality of doing wrong, the possibility of doing evil. And it is by his will that man is tempted to be as a god, to be more than a man within mankind, to be a man over other men, to control them.

In the physical world in which he lives, there would be no evil without man, only change — grass and trees, fishes and mammals, living by instinct and genetic direction, transferring energy one to the other and then passing on in decay. In this world about him that obeys and fulfills the laws and constructs of physics and chemistry, man is marked not by his logic, but by his will. Only man, by his own willful acts, is capable of doing that most illogical of things — hurting himself, making himself unhappy.

Man has had a will since the beginning of time. In fact, it was when he was given a will that human time began. It is in time that our will is engaged, finds expression. It is in time that there is fear; it is time that there is hope. Without time, our will would have no meaning for it is in time that there is consequence to our acts. And it is in seeking to live beyond time that we find fulfillment. What is art — music, painting, the flight of the unbridled athlete — if it does not suspend time, remove us from it, free us of it? What is love if not being, within ourselves, unafraid, unaware of time and its consequence? It is in time that there is the fear of death and it is in being beyond time that there is the fulfillment of life — happiness.

So this is the challenge — to keep our will and to escape time. To do this, keys are needed, things apart from the goal that will take us to it, keys that are unique in origin and application to each of us. For my part, I have discovered four: faith, courage, discipline and patience. These are, each of them, things of the will. I do not claim to have these at all times, or even any one of them most of the time. It has been enough to know that I need them, for it is in knowing that I need them that I know I can have them — through my will.

Faith

Faith has to do with believing, with knowing that which you cannot see or touch. Faith is a commitment to look for the good in a thing and to go on from there. It is how things get better. Faith is the belief that any life lived to be better is already better — is something good and of value. It is an understanding that you don't lose when you are defeated, only when you quit. Faith starts first with finding the good in yourself and then believing that the things and people around you are the better for it. It has to do with seizing life's force and willing your way into the future. Faith is escaping what has gone before. Having faith is putting time on your side.

Courage

Courage is not so much a spontaneous act of daring in a moment of high drama. It is a more common thing. Courage is what we must have if we are to live a good life each day, every day — to be a good mother or a good father or a good child or friend. It takes courage to do the right thing — for ourselves and for those around us. There is in each of us a course set by what we want to be, by how we want to act, by our values, by the things we see as the good in us. And it is by courage that we stay this course, by which we will it to happen. It is a conscious act, a commitment to do the good as we see it. Being a good person is not easy until you are one (and not always then) and you can't be one without courage.

Discipline

Discipline is an understanding that you can control your needs and then deciding to do it. It means setting your own rules within those of society and keeping to them. With discipline, the hard choices come easier — and need be made only once. Without discipline, you become mired in indecision and doubt. Discipline starts with the small things and then builds across your daily life. With discipline, you can separate that which you really need from among those things that you merely want. Without discipline, you get what is provided, what is made available to you by others. With discipline, everything you *need,* literally, can be yours.

Patience

Patience means having the strength to give things time to go your way. It's what you get when you have the other three.

. . . and remember this above all else
The one life you have been given is a miracle
Live it Joyfully.

About the Author

P.D. St. Claire is the pen name of a Washington, D. C. executive recruiter.

A native of Long Island, New York, he moved to Washington in 1968 where he spent 12 years with U. S. Government before joining a national trade association as an international economist. Other works include two novels, St. Patrick's Day, A Love Story and Saigon Passage. A resident of Kensington, MD, he lives with his wife of 32 years, Michaele Anne. They have three grown children and a dog.

CPSIA information can be obtained
at www.ICGtesting.com
Printed in the USA
JSHW050745010621
15333JS00001B/56